Contents

D0483006

Chocolate Graham Cracker Sundae

- $1\frac{3}{4}$ graham crackers
- 2 tablespoons marshmallow crème
- 2 scoops (about $\frac{1}{4}$ cup each) vanilla ice cream
- 2 tablespoons HERSHEY'S Syrup
- $\frac{1}{4}$ cup miniature marshmallows

PLACE 2 halves of graham crackers in bottom of chilled bowl.

SPOON marshmallow crème onto each half graham cracker.

PLACE scoops of vanilla ice cream onto the marshmallow crème.

TOP ice cream with chocolate syrup.

FAN the remaining three quarters of graham cracker in between the scoops of ice cream.

SPRINKLE the marshmallows onto the chocolate syrup around the ice cream.

Makes 1 serving

Black and White Sundae

- 1 to 2 chocolate wafer cookies
- 2 to 3 tablespoons HERSHEY'S Syrup
- 1 scoop (about ½ cup) chocolate ice cream, softened
- ½ cup HERSHEY'S MINI KISSES BRAND Milk Chocolates
- 1 scoop (about ½ cup) vanilla ice cream, softened
- 1 tablespoon HERSHEY'S Cocoa or HERSHEY'S SPECIAL DARK Cocoa (optional)
- 1 tablespoon powdered sugar (optional)

CRUSH cookies; place on bottom of ice cream dish. Cover cookies with syrup.

COMBINE 1 scoop chocolate ice cream with chocolate pieces; place on top of cookies and syrup. Top with scoop vanilla ice cream.

STIR together cocoa and powdered sugar, if desired. Sprinkle over ice cream. Garnish as desired.

Makes 1 serving

Mocha Chocolate Chip Cookies

- 2½ cups all-purpose flour
- 1 teaspoon salt
- 1 teaspoon baking soda
- 1 teaspoon ground cinnamon
- 1 cup (2 sticks) butter or margarine, softened
- 1 cup packed light brown sugar
- ½ cup granulated sugar
- 2 tablespoons HERSHEY'S SPECIAL DARK Syrup
- 1½ teaspoons vanilla extract
- 2 eggs
- 1½ teaspoons powdered instant coffee or espresso, dissolved in 1 teaspoon hot water
- 2 cups (12-ounce package) HERSHEY'S SPECIAL DARK Chocolate Chips
- 1½ cups chopped pecans

HEAT oven to 350°F. Line cookie sheet with parchment paper.

STIR together flour, salt, baking soda and cinnamon. Beat butter, brown sugar, granulated sugar, chocolate syrup and vanilla in large bowl with mixer until creamy. Add eggs and coffee; beat well. Gradually add flour mixture, beating well. Stir in chocolate chips and pecans. Drop by rounded teaspoons about 2 inches apart onto prepared cookie sheet.

BAKE 10 to 12 minutes or until lightly browned. Cool slightly; remove from cookie sheet to wire rack. Cool completely.

Makes about 5 dozen cookies

Chocolate Brownies Deluxe

- ½ cup (1 stick) butter or margarine, softened
- 1 cup sugar
- 2 eggs
- 1 teaspoon vanilla extract
- 1¼ cups all-purpose flour
- ¼ cup HERSHEY'S Cocoa
- ¼ teaspoon baking soda
- ¾ cup HERSHEY'S Syrup
- 1 cup REESE'S Peanut Butter Chips
- FUDGE BROWNIE FROSTING (recipe follows)

HEAT oven to 350°F. Grease 13×9×2-inch baking pan.

BEAT butter, sugar, eggs and vanilla in large bowl until fluffy. Stir together flour, cocoa and baking soda; add alternately with syrup to butter mixture, beating well after each addition. Stir in peanut butter chips. Spread batter in prepared pan.

BAKE 40 to 45 minutes or until brownies begin to pull away from sides of pan. Cool completely in pan on wire rack. Prepare FUDGE BROWNIE FROSTING; spread over brownies. Cut into bars.

Makes about 24 brownies

FUDGE BROWNIE FROSTING

- 3 tablespoons butter or margarine, softened
- 3 tablespoons HERSHEY'S Cocoa
- 1 cup powdered sugar
- 1 tablespoon milk
- ¾ teaspoon vanilla extract

BEAT butter and cocoa in small bowl until well blended; gradually add powdered sugar alternately with combined milk and vanilla, beating until smooth and of spreading consistency. Add additional milk, ½ teaspoon at a time, if needed.

Makes about 1 cup frosting

Chocolate Indulgence

- 1 chocolate fudge brownie
- 1 scoop (about ½ cup) chocolate ice cream
- 2 tablespoons HERSHEY'S Syrup
- Whipped cream
- 1 tablespoon HERSHEY'S Milk Chocolate Chips

PLACE brownie in sundae dish; top with scoop of chocolate ice cream.

DRIZZLE syrup over ice cream and brownie. Garnish with whipped cream and milk chocolate chips.

Makes 1 serving

Double Peanut Butter Paisley Brownies

- 1/2 cup (1 stick) butter or margarine, softened
- 1/4 cup REESE'S Creamy Peanut Butter
- 1 cup granulated sugar
- 1 cup packed light brown sugar
- 3 eggs
- 1 teaspoon vanilla extract
- 2 cups all-purpose flour
- 2 teaspoons baking powder
- 1/4 teaspoon salt
- 1 2/3 cups (10-ounce package) REESE'S Peanut Butter Chips
- 1/2 cup HERSHEY'S Syrup or HERSHEY'S SPECIAL DARK Syrup

HEAT oven to 350°F. Grease 13×9×2-inch baking pan.

BEAT butter and peanut butter in large bowl. Add granulated sugar and brown sugar; beat well. Add eggs, one at a time, beating well after each addition. Blend in vanilla.

STIR together flour, baking powder and salt; mix into peanut butter mixture, blending well. Stir in peanut butter chips. Spread half of batter in prepared pan; spoon syrup over top. Carefully top with remaining batter; swirl with metal spatula or knife for marbled effect.

BAKE 35 to 40 minutes or until lightly browned. Cool completely in pan on wire rack. Cut into squares.

Makes about 36 brownies

Fudgey Fruit Pizza

- ½ cup (1 stick) lower fat vegetable oil spread
- ¾ cup granulated sugar
- 2 teaspoons vanilla extract, divided
- ½ cup plus 1 tablespoon HERSHEY'S Cocoa, divided
- 1¼ cups all-purpose flour
- ½ cup HERSHEY'S Syrup, divided
- 1 package (8 ounces) nonfat cream cheese
- 1 cup powdered sugar
- 2 cups sliced fresh fruit
- ¼ cup HERSHEY'S Strawberry Syrup

HEAT oven to 325°F. Lightly grease 12-inch pizza pan.

BEAT vegetable oil spread, granulated sugar and 1 teaspoon vanilla until creamy. Add ½ cup cocoa; beat well. Gradually add flour and ¼ cup chocolate syrup, beating until well combined. Press dough evenly into prepared pan, forming cookie crust. Bake 20 to 25 minutes or until set. Cool completely.

PREPARE filling by combining cream cheese, powdered sugar, remaining 1 tablespoon cocoa and remaining 1 teaspoon vanilla extract. Spread over crust to within 1 inch of edge. Cover; refrigerate until cold, about 1 hour.

JUST before serving, place sliced fruit on top; drizzle with remaining ¼ cup chocolate syrup and strawberry syrup. Serve immediately, cut into slices.

Makes 12 servings

HERSHEY'S Syrup Snacking Brownies

- ½ cup (1 stick) butter or margarine, softened
- 1 cup sugar
- 1½ cups HERSHEY'S Syrup*
- 4 eggs
- 1¼ cups all-purpose flour
- 1 cup HERSHEY'S SPECIAL DARK Chocolate Chips or HERSHEY'S Semi-Sweet Chocolate Chips

**One 16-ounce can HERSHEY'S Syrup contains 1½ cups syrup.*

HEAT oven to 350°F. Grease 13×9×2-inch baking pan.

BEAT butter and sugar in large bowl. Add syrup, eggs and flour; beat well. Stir in chocolate chips. Pour batter into prepared pan.

BAKE 30 to 35 minutes or until brownies begin to pull away from sides of pan. Cool completely in pan on wire rack. Cut into bars.

Makes about 36 brownies

Classic HERSHEY'S Bar Cake

- 1 cup (2 sticks) butter or margarine, softened
- 1¼ cups granulated sugar
- 4 eggs
- 6 HERSHEY'S Milk Chocolate Bars (1.55 ounces each), melted
- 2½ cups all-purpose flour
- ¼ teaspoon baking soda
- Dash salt
- 1 cup buttermilk or sour milk*
- ½ cup HERSHEY'S Syrup
- 2 teaspoons vanilla extract
- 1 cup chopped pecans
- Powdered sugar (optional)

**To sour milk: Use 1 tablespoon white vinegar plus milk to equal 1 cup.*

HEAT oven to 350°F. Grease and flour 10-inch tube pan or 12-cup fluted tube pan.

BEAT butter in large bowl until creamy; gradually add granulated sugar, beating on medium speed of mixer until well blended. Add eggs, one at a time, beating well after each addition. Add chocolate; beat until blended.

STIR together flour, baking soda and salt; add to chocolate mixture alternately with buttermilk, beating until blended. Add syrup and vanilla; beat until blended. Stir in pecans. Pour batter into prepared pan.

BAKE 1 hour and 15 minutes or until wooden pick inserted in center of cake comes out clean. Cool 10 minutes; remove from pan to wire rack. Cool completely. Sift powdered sugar over top, if desired.

Makes 12 to 16 servings

Neapolitan Delight Cake

- 27 ladyfingers, split
- 3 packages (3 ounces each) cream cheese, softened and divided
- 2/3 cup HERSHEY'S Syrup or HERSHEY'S SPECIAL DARK Syrup
- 1/3 cup plus 1/4 cup water, divided
- 5 1/4 cups light frozen whipped topping, thawed and divided
- 1/3 cup HERSHEY'S Strawberry Syrup
- Whipped topping (optional)
- Sliced strawberries (optional)

LINE 9-inch springform pan with foil; place ladyfingers, cut sides in, to fit on bottom and around sides of prepared pan.

BEAT half of cream cheese in small bowl until fluffy; gradually blend in chocolate syrup and 1/3 cup water until smooth. Fold in 2 1/2 cups topping until blended; spread evenly over ladyfingers. Cut rounded ends off remaining ladyfingers; place to fit over top of chocolate layer.

BEAT remaining half of cream cheese in small bowl until fluffy; gradually blend in strawberry syrup and remaining 1/4 cup water. Fold in remaining 2 3/4 cups topping until blended; spread evenly over ladyfingers. Cover; freeze 6 hours or until firm.

REMOVE foil; garnish with whipped topping and sliced strawberries, if desired. Serve frozen, cut into slices.

Makes 12 to 16 servings

Chocolate Mousse Cake Roll

CHOCOLATE MOUSSE FILLING (recipe follows)
- 4 eggs, separated
- ½ cup plus ⅓ cup granulated sugar, divided
- 1 teaspoon vanilla extract
- ½ cup all-purpose flour
- ⅓ cup HERSHEY'S Cocoa
- ½ teaspoon baking powder
- ¼ teaspoon baking soda
- ⅛ teaspoon salt
- ⅓ cup water

Powdered sugar
HERSHEY'S Syrup

PREPARE CHOCOLATE MOUSSE FILLING. Chill 6 to 8 hours or overnight.

PREPARE cake.* Heat oven to 375°F. Line 15½×10½×1-inch jelly-roll pan with foil; generously grease foil.

BEAT egg whites in large bowl until soft peaks form; gradually add ½ cup granulated sugar, beating until stiff peaks form. Beat egg yolks and vanilla in medium bowl on medium speed of mixer 3 minutes. Gradually add remaining ⅓ cup granulated sugar; continue beating 2 additional minutes.

STIR together flour, cocoa, baking powder, baking soda and salt; add to egg yolk mixture alternately with water, beating on low speed just until batter is smooth. Gradually fold chocolate mixture into beaten egg whites until well blended. Spread batter evenly in prepared pan.

BAKE 12 to 15 minutes or until top springs back when touched lightly in center. Immediately loosen cake from edges of pan; invert onto clean towel sprinkled with powdered sugar. Carefully peel off foil. Immediately roll cake and towel together starting from narrow end; place on wire rack to cool completely.

CAREFULLY unroll cake; remove towel. Gently stir filling until of spreading consistency. Spread cake with CHOCOLATE MOUSSE FILLING; reroll cake. Refrigerate several hours. Sift powdered sugar over top just before serving. Serve drizzled with syrup

and garnished as desired. Cover; refrigerate leftover cake roll.

**Cake may be prepared up to two days in advance. Keep cake rolled tightly and covered well so that it doesn't get dry.*

Makes 8 to 10 servings

CHOCOLATE MOUSSE FILLING

- ¼ cup sugar
- 1 teaspoon unflavored gelatin
- ½ cup milk
- 1 cup HERSHEY'S SPECIAL DARK Chocolate Chips or HERSHEY'S Semi-Sweet Chocolate Chips
- 2 teaspoons vanilla extract
- 1 cup (½ pint) cold whipping cream

STIR together sugar and gelatin in small saucepan; stir in milk. Let stand 2 minutes to soften gelatin. Cook over medium heat, stirring constantly, until mixture just begins to boil.

REMOVE from heat. Immediately add chocolate chips; stir until melted. Stir in vanilla; cool to room temperature.

BEAT whipping cream in small bowl until stiff. Gradually add chocolate mixture, folding gently just until blended. Cover; refrigerate until ready to use.

Makes about 3 cups

Chocolate Cappuccino Cream Cake

- 27 ladyfingers, split
- 3 packages (3 ounces each) cream cheese, softened and divided
- ⅔ cup plus 2 tablespoons HERSHEY'S Syrup or HERSHEY'S SPECIAL DARK Syrup, divided
- ⅓ cup water
- 5¼ cups frozen whipped topping, thawed and divided
- ½ cup cold brewed coffee

LINE 9-inch springform pan with foil; place ladyfingers, cut side in, to fit on bottom and around sides of prepared pan.

BEAT half of cream cheese until fluffy in medium bowl; gradually blend in ⅔ cup chocolate syrup and ⅓ cup water until smooth. Fold in 2½ cups topping until blended; spread evenly over ladyfingers. Cut rounded ends off remaining ladyfingers; place to fit over top of chocolate layer.

BEAT remaining half of cream cheese until fluffy in medium bowl; gradually blend in cold coffee and remaining 2 tablespoons chocolate syrup. Fold in remaining 2¾ cups topping until blended; spread evenly over ladyfingers. Cover; freeze 6 hours or until firm.

REMOVE foil; garnish, if desired. Serve frozen, cut into slices.

Makes 12 to 16 servings

Chocolate Syrup Swirl Cake

- 1 cup (2 sticks) butter or margarine, softened
- 2 cups sugar
- 2 teaspoons vanilla extract
- 3 eggs
- 2¾ cups all-purpose flour
- 1¼ teaspoons baking soda, divided
- ½ teaspoon salt
- 1 cup buttermilk or sour milk*
- 1 cup HERSHEY'S Syrup
- 1 cup MOUNDS Sweetened Coconut Flakes (optional)

**To sour milk: Use 1 tablespoon white vinegar plus milk to equal 1 cup.*

HEAT oven to 350°F. Grease and flour a 12-cup fluted tube pan or 10-inch tube pan.

BEAT butter, sugar and vanilla in large bowl until fluffy. Add eggs; beat well. Stir together flour, 1 teaspoon baking soda and salt; add alternately with buttermilk to butter mixture, beating until well blended.

MEASURE 2 cups batter in small bowl; stir in syrup and remaining ¼ teaspoon baking soda. Add coconut, if desired, to remaining vanilla batter; pour into prepared pan. Pour chocolate batter over vanilla batter in pan; do not mix.

BAKE 60 to 70 minutes or until wooden pick inserted in center comes out clean. Cool 15 minutes; remove from pan to wire rack. Cool completely; glaze or frost as desired.

Makes 20 servings

Chocolate Strawberry Whipped Cream Cake

- 3 eggs
- 1 cup granulated sugar
- 1/3 cup water
- 1 teaspoon vanilla extract
- 3/4 cup all-purpose flour
- 1/4 cup HERSHEY'S Cocoa or HERSHEY'S SPECIAL DARK Cocoa
- 1 teaspoon baking powder
- 1/2 teaspoon salt
- Powdered sugar
- STRAWBERRY WHIPPED CREAM FILLING (recipe follows)
- ROYAL GLAZE (recipe follows)

HEAT oven to 375°F. Grease 15½×10½×1-inch jelly-roll pan. Line with wax paper; grease paper.

BEAT eggs in large bowl on high speed of mixer until very thick and cream colored, about 5 minutes; gradually beat in granulated sugar. With mixer on low speed, beat in water and vanilla. Stir together flour, cocoa, baking powder and salt; gradually add to egg mixture, beating just until blended. Pour into prepared pan.

BAKE 10 to 13 minutes or until wooden pick inserted in center comes out clean. Immediately invert pan onto towel sprinkled with powdered sugar; carefully peel off wax paper. Invert cake onto wire rack covered with wax paper. Cool completely.

PREPARE STRAWBERRY WHIPPED CREAM FILLING. Cut cake crosswise into four equal pieces, each about 10×3½ inches. Divide filling into thirds; spread evenly on three rectangles, leaving one plain rectangle for top. Cover and refrigerate until firm. To assemble, stack layers on top of each other with plain cake layer on top. Prepare ROYAL GLAZE; spread over top. Refrigerate until serving. Cut into slices; refrigerate leftover cake.

Makes 8 to 10 servings

STRAWBERRY WHIPPED CREAM FILLING

- 1 cup rinsed, hulled and sliced fresh strawberries
- 1/4 cup HERSHEY'S Strawberry Syrup
- 1 envelope unflavored gelatin
- 1 cup (1/2 pint) cold whipping cream

PURÉE strawberries with syrup in food processor or blender; sprinkle gelatin over mixture. Let stand until gelatin is softened, about 2 minutes; purée again for several seconds. Pour into medium microwave-safe bowl; microwave at HIGH (100%) 30 seconds to 1 minute, until mixture is hot, not boiling, and gelatin is dissolved. Cool to room temperature (about 30 minutes), stirring occasionally.

BEAT whipping cream in small bowl on high speed of mixer until stiff; fold in strawberry mixture.

ROYAL GLAZE

- 2/3 cup HERSHEY'S SPECIAL DARK Chocolate Chips or HERSHEY'S Semi-Sweet Chocolate Chips
- 1/4 cup whipping cream

PLACE chocolate chips and whipping cream in small microwave-safe bowl. Microwave at MEDIUM (50%) 30 seconds; stir. If necessary, microwave at MEDIUM an additional 10 seconds at a time, stirring after each heating, just until chips are melted when stirred. Cool slightly until thickened, 5 to 10 minutes.

White Chip and Coconut Chocolate Swirl Cake

- 1 cup (2 sticks) butter or margarine, softened
- 2 cups sugar
- 2 teaspoons vanilla extract
- 3 eggs
- 2¾ cups all-purpose flour
- 1¼ teaspoons baking soda, divided
- ½ teaspoon salt
- 1 cup buttermilk or sour milk*
- 1 cup HERSHEY'S Syrup
- 1 cup HERSHEY'S Premier White Chips
- 1 cup MOUNDS Sweetened Coconut Flakes

**To sour milk: Use 1 tablespoon white vinegar plus milk to equal 1 cup.*

HEAT oven to 350°F. Grease and flour 12-cup fluted tube pan or 10-inch tube pan.

BEAT butter, sugar and vanilla in large bowl until fluffy. Add eggs; beat well. Stir together flour, 1 teaspoon baking soda and salt; add alternately with buttermilk to butter mixture, beating until well blended.

MEASURE 2 cups batter into small bowl; stir in syrup and remaining ¼ teaspoon baking soda. Add white chips and coconut to remaining batter; pour into prepared pan. Spoon chocolate batter over vanilla batter in pan; do not mix.

BAKE 65 to 75 minutes or until wooden pick inserted in center comes out clean. (Cake will sink in the center.) Cool 15 minutes; remove from pan to wire rack. Cool completely; glaze or frost as desired.

Makes 20 servings

HERSHEY'S One-Bowl Syrup Cake

- ½ cup (1 stick) butter or margarine, softened
- 1 cup sugar
- 4 eggs
- 1¼ cups all-purpose flour
- ¼ teaspoon baking soda
- 1½ cups HERSHEY'S Syrup*

One 16-ounce can HERSHEY'S Syrup contains 1½ cups syrup.

HEAT oven to 350°F. Grease 13×9×2-inch baking pan.

BEAT butter, sugar and eggs until thoroughly blended in large bowl. Add flour and baking soda, blending well. Add syrup; mix thoroughly. Spread batter in prepared pan.

BAKE 35 to 40 minutes or until wooden pick inserted in center of cake comes out clean. Cool completely in pan on wire rack. Frost and garnish as desired.

Makes 8 to 10 servings

Milk Chocolate Tres Leche Cake

- ½ cup (1 stick) butter, softened
- 1 cup sugar
- 5 eggs
- 2 teaspoons vanilla extract
- 1⅓ cups cake flour
- ⅓ cup HERSHEY'S Cocoa
- 1 teaspoon baking powder
- ½ teaspoon salt
- TRES LECHE GLAZE (recipe follows)
- CREAM TOPPING (recipe follows)

HEAT oven to 350°F. Grease and flour 13×9×2-inch baking pan.

BEAT butter in large bowl with electric mixer until light and fluffy. Gradually beat in sugar, continuing to beat about 1 minute. Add eggs, one at a time, beating well after each addition. Blend in vanilla. Stir together flour, cocoa, baking powder and salt. Gradually blend flour mixture into butter mixture, mixing just until blended. Pour batter into prepared pan.

BAKE 20 to 25 minutes or until golden brown and wooden pick inserted in center comes out clean. Cool cake in pan on wire rack for 30 minutes. With skewer or fork, pierce the entire top of the cake. Prepare TRES LECHE GLAZE. Reserve 1½ cups glaze; pour remaining glaze over cake. Cover; refrigerate cake and reserved glaze overnight. (Cake should absorb most of the glaze and will be very wet.)

PREPARE CREAM TOPPING. Spread topping over cake; refrigerate until ready to serve. To serve, pour 1 to 2 tablespoons of the reserved glaze onto bottom of each individual dessert dish. Place cake piece on this glaze. Garnish as desired. Cover; refrigerate leftovers.

Tres Leche Glaze: Stir together 2 cans (14 ounces each) sweetened condensed milk, 1 can (12 ounces) evaporated milk, 1 cup heavy cream and ¾ cup HERSHEY'S Syrup in pitcher or large bowl.

Cream Topping: Beat 2 cups (1 pint) whipping cream, 1 cup sugar, ¼ cup HERSHEY'S Cocoa and 1 teaspoon vanilla extract in large mixing bowl until stiff.

Makes 12 to 16 servings

Easy Fudgey Pudding Cake

- 1 cup all-purpose biscuit baking mix
- ¼ cup HERSHEY'S Cocoa
- 1 can (14 ounces) sweetened condensed milk (not evaporated milk), divided
- ¾ cup HERSHEY'S Syrup, divided
- 1 teaspoon vanilla extract
- ¾ cup hot water
- Whipped topping or ice cream (optional)

HEAT oven to 375°F. Grease 8-inch square baking pan.

COMBINE baking mix and cocoa in medium bowl; stir in 1 cup sweetened condensed milk, ¼ cup syrup and vanilla until blended. Spoon evenly into prepared pan.

COMBINE remaining sweetened condensed milk, remaining ½ cup syrup and water in small bowl. Pour liquid mixture carefully over top of mixture in pan; do not stir.

BAKE 25 to 30 minutes or until center is set and cake begins to pull away from sides of pan. Let stand 10 minutes; spoon into dessert dishes, spooning pudding from bottom of pan over top. Serve warm; garnish with whipped topping, if desired. Cover; refrigerate leftover dessert.

Makes 6 to 8 servings

Neapolitan Ice Cream Sandwich Cake

- 1 frozen loaf pound cake ($10^3/_4$ ounces), partially thawed
- 2 cups (1 pint) vanilla ice cream, slightly softened and divided
- 2 tablespoons HERSHEY'S Strawberry Syrup
- 2 tablespoons HERSHEY'S Syrup or HERSHEY'S SPECIAL DARK Syrup

REMOVE cake from foil pan; line pan with plastic wrap. With serrated knife, slice cake horizontally into 3 layers; place bottom cake layer into prepared pan and place in freezer.

STIR together 1 cup ice cream and strawberry syrup in small bowl; spread over cake layer in pan. Gently place second cake layer on top of strawberry mixture; immediately return to freezer.

STIR together remaining 1 cup ice cream and chocolate syrup in small bowl; spread over cake layer in pan. Top with third cake layer; cover and freeze until firm.

SERVE frozen, cut into slices. Cover; freeze leftover cake.

Makes about 8 servings

Easy Peanut Butter Cake

- $1\frac{2}{3}$ cups (10-ounce package) REESE'S Peanut Butter Chips
- 1 tablespoon shortening (do not use butter, margarine, spread or oil)
- 1 package (about 18 ounces) regular white or yellow cake mix (not pudding-in-mix type)
- PEANUT BUTTER WHIPPED CREAM FROSTING (recipe follows)
- HERSHEY'S Syrup
- Chocolate curls (optional)

HEAT oven to 350°F. Grease and wax paper-line two 8- or 9-inch round baking pans.

PLACE peanut butter chips and shortening in medium microwave-safe bowl. Microwave at MEDIUM (50%) $1\frac{1}{2}$ minutes or until smooth when stirred. Prepare cake mix as directed on package; blend in melted chip mixture. Pour batter into prepared pans.

BAKE 30 to 35 minutes or until wooden pick inserted in center comes out clean. Cool 10 minutes; remove from pans to wire racks. Cool completely.

FROST with PEANUT BUTTER WHIPPED CREAM FROSTING. Refrigerate until serving time. Serve with syrup drizzled over top and sides of cake. Garnish with chocolate curls, if desired. Cover; refrigerate leftover cake.

Variation: Cake may be baked in greased and floured 13×9×2-inch baking pan. Bake 30 to 35 minutes or until wooden pick inserted in center of cake comes out clean. Cool completely in pan on wire rack. Frost with ½ recipe PEANUT BUTTER WHIPPED CREAM FROSTING.

Makes 10 to 12 servings

PEANUT BUTTER WHIPPED CREAM FROSTING

- $1\frac{2}{3}$ cups (10-ounce package) REESE'S Peanut Butter Chips
- ⅔ cup milk
- 3 cups miniature marshmallows
- 2 cups (1 pint) cold whipping cream
- ½ teaspoon vanilla extract

STIR together peanut butter chips, milk and marshmallows in 2-quart saucepan. Heat over low heat, stirring constantly, until chips and marshmallows are melted and mixture is smooth; cool to lukewarm. Beat whipping cream in small bowl with electric mixer until stiff; fold in vanilla and cooled peanut butter chip mixture.

Makes about 4 cups frosting

Pears in Paradise

- **2 tablespoons HERSHEY'S Syrup**
- **½ cup vanilla ice cream**
- **1 to 2 tablespoons HERSHEY'S Caramel Topping**
- **1 pear half, canned**
- **½ teaspoon cinnamon-sugar**
- **⅓ cup additional HERSHEY'S Syrup**
- **Whipped cream**
- **2 teaspoons toasted pecan pieces***

**To toast pecans: Heat oven to 350°F. Place pecans in single layer in shallow baking pan. Bake 7 to 8 minutes, stirring occasionally, until light brown. Cool completely.*

POUR 2 tablespoons chocolate syrup into bottom of chilled bowl or stemmed dessert glass. Top with ice cream; drizzle with caramel topping.

PLACE pear half on caramel; sprinkle with cinnamon-sugar. Drizzle with additional ⅓ cup chocolate syrup. Garnish with whipped cream rosettes and toasted pecans.

Makes 1 (10-ounce) serving

Fudge Walnut Brownie Pie

- 2 eggs
- 1 cup sugar
- ½ cup (1 stick) butter, melted
- 1 teaspoon vanilla extract
- ⅔ cup all-purpose flour
- ⅓ cup HERSHEY'S Cocoa
- ¼ teaspoon salt
- 1 cup HERSHEY'S SPECIAL DARK Chocolate Chips or HERSHEY'S Semi-Sweet Chocolate Chips
- ½ cup chopped walnuts
- Ice cream
- HERSHEY'S Syrup

HEAT oven to 350°F. Lightly grease 9-inch pie plate.

BEAT eggs in large bowl; stir in sugar, butter and vanilla. Stir together flour, cocoa and salt; stir into butter mixture. Stir in chocolate chips and walnuts. Pour into prepared pie plate.

BAKE 30 to 35 minutes or until set. Cool. Serve warm or at room temperature with ice cream; drizzle syrup over top.

Makes 6 to 8 servings

Note: In place of pie plate, batter can be baked in lightly greased 8-inch square baking pan. Bake at 350°F for 30 to 35 minutes or until brownies begin to pull away from sides of pan.

Chocolate Raspberry Dessert

- 1 cup all-purpose flour
- 1 cup sugar
- ½ cup (1 stick) butter or margarine, softened
- ¼ teaspoon baking powder
- 4 eggs
- 1½ cups HERSHEY'S Syrup*
- RASPBERRY CREAM CENTER (recipe follows)
- CHOCOLATE GLAZE (recipe follows)

**One 16-ounce can HERSHEY'S Syrup contains 1½ cups syrup.*

HEAT oven to 350°F. Grease 13×9×2-inch baking pan.

COMBINE flour, sugar, butter, baking powder and eggs in large bowl; beat until smooth. Add syrup; blend thoroughly. Pour batter into prepared pan.

BAKE 25 to 30 minutes or until wooden pick inserted in center comes out clean. Cool completely in pan on wire rack. Spread RASPBERRY CREAM CENTER on cake. Cover; refrigerate. Pour CHOCOLATE GLAZE over chilled dessert. Cover; refrigerate at least 1 hour before serving. Cover; refrigerate leftover dessert.

Raspberry Cream Center: Combine 2 cups powdered sugar, ½ cup (1 stick) softened butter or margarine and 2 tablespoons raspberry-flavored liqueur** in small bowl; beat until smooth. (A few drops red food coloring may be added, if desired.)

***¼ cup raspberry preserves mixed with 1 teaspoon water may be substituted for the raspberry-flavored liqueur.*

Chocolate Glaze: Melt 6 tablespoons butter or margarine and 1 cup HERSHEY'S SPECIAL DARK Chocolate Chips or HERSHEY'S Semi-Sweet Chocolate Chips in small saucepan over very low heat. Remove from heat; stir until smooth. Cool slightly.

Makes about 12 servings

Chocolate Ice Crispy Pie

- ½ cup HERSHEY'S Syrup
- ⅓ cup HERSHEY'S SPECIAL DARK Chocolate Chips or HERSHEY'S Semi-Sweet Chocolate Chips
- 2 cups crisp rice cereal
- 4 cups (1 quart) your favorite flavor ice cream
- Additional HERSHEY'S Syrup

BUTTER 9-inch pie plate.

PLACE syrup and chocolate chips in medium microwave-safe bowl. Microwave at MEDIUM (50%) 45 seconds or until hot; stir until smooth. Remove ¼ cup chocolate mixture to small bowl; set aside. Add cereal to remaining chocolate mixture, stirring until well coated; cool slightly.

USING back of spoon, press mixture evenly on bottom and up sides of prepared pie plate to form crust. Place in freezer 15 to 20 minutes or until crust is firm. Spread one-half of ice cream into crust; spoon chocolate sauce over layer. Top with scoops of remaining ice cream. Cover; return to freezer until serving time. Drizzle with additional chocolate syrup just before serving.

Makes 8 servings

Coconut-Cereal Crust: Decrease cereal to 1¾ cups; add ½ cup MOUNDS Sweetened Coconut Flakes.

Chocolate Bavarian Pie

- 1 envelope unflavored gelatin
- $1\frac{3}{4}$ cups milk, divided
- $\frac{2}{3}$ cup sugar
- 6 tablespoons HERSHEY'S Cocoa
- 1 tablespoon light corn syrup
- 2 tablespoons butter
- $\frac{3}{4}$ teaspoon vanilla extract
- 1 cup ($\frac{1}{2}$ pint) cold whipping cream
- 1 baked 9-inch pie crust or crumb crust
- HERSHEY'S Syrup

SPRINKLE gelatin over 1 cup milk in medium saucepan; let stand 2 minutes to soften.

STIR together sugar and cocoa; add to milk mixture. Add corn syrup. Cook, stirring constantly, until mixture boils. Remove from heat. Add butter; stir until melted. Stir in remaining $\frac{3}{4}$ cup milk and vanilla. Pour into large bowl. Cool; refrigerate until almost set.

BEAT whipping cream in small bowl on high speed of mixer until stiff. Beat chocolate mixture on medium speed until smooth. On low speed, add whipped cream to chocolate mixture, beating just until blended. Pour into prepared crust; refrigerate* until set, at least 3 hours. Just before serving, drizzle each pie slice with chocolate syrup. Cover; refrigerate leftover pie.

Makes 8 servings

**FROZEN CHOCOLATE BAVARIAN PIE: Freeze pie 4 to 6 hours or overnight. Remove from freezer 10 to 15 minutes before serving.*

Chocolate Cup Brownie Sundae

6 **CHOCOLATE SHELLS (recipe follows)**
Brownie pieces
Ice cream (any flavor)
HERSHEY'S Syrup
Strawberries, blueberries or other fresh fruit slices
Whipped topping or sweetened whipped cream

PREPARE CHOCOLATE SHELLS at least 2 hours in advance.

REMOVE foil from outside of chocolate shell for each sundae. Place brownie pieces in bottom of chocolate shell. Top with ice cream. Garnish with syrup, fresh fruit and whipped topping.

Makes 6 cups

Chocolate Shells:
LINE 6 muffin cups (2½ inches in diameter) with foil or paper baking cups. Place 24 unwrapped HERSHEY'S KISSESBRAND Milk Chocolates (or ⅔ cup HERSHEY'S MINI KISSESBRAND Milk Chocolates) or HERSHEY'S KISSESBRAND SPECIAL DARK Mildly Sweet Chocolates in medium microwave-safe bowl. Microwave at MEDIUM (50%) 1 minute; stir. If necessary, microwave at MEDIUM an additional 15 seconds at a time, stirring after each heating, until chocolates are melted and smooth when stirred. Cool slightly.

COAT inside of pleated surfaces and bottom of bake cups thickly and evenly with melted chocolate using a soft-bristled pastry brush. Refrigerate coated cups 10 minutes or until set; recoat any thin spots with melted chocolate. (If necessary, reheat chocolate at MEDIUM for a few seconds.) Refrigerate cups until very firm, 2 hours or overnight. Cover; refrigerate until ready to use.

Crispy Chocolate Ice Cream Mud Pie

- ½ cup HERSHEY'S Syrup
- ⅓ cup HERSHEY'S SPECIAL DARK Chocolate Chips or HERSHEY'S Semi-Sweet Chocolate Chips
- 2 cups crisp rice cereal
- 4 cups (1 quart) vanilla ice cream, divided
- 4 cups (1 quart) chocolate ice cream, divided
- Additional HERSHEY'S Syrup

BUTTER 9-inch pie plate.

PLACE ½ cup chocolate syrup and chocolate chips in medium microwave-safe bowl. Microwave at MEDIUM (50%) 45 seconds or until hot; stir until smooth. Reserve ¼ cup chocolate syrup mixture; set aside. Add cereal to remaining chocolate syrup mixture, stirring until well coated; cool slightly.

PRESS cereal mixture, using back of spoon, evenly on bottom and up side of prepared pie plate to form crust. Place in freezer 15 to 20 minutes or until crust is firm. Spread half of vanilla ice cream into crust; spoon reserved ¼ cup chocolate syrup mixture over layer. Spread half of chocolate ice cream over sauce.

TOP with alternating scoops of vanilla and chocolate ice cream. Cover; return to freezer until serving time. Drizzle with additional chocolate syrup just before serving.

Makes 8 servings

Our Gal Sundae Pie

MACAROON-NUT CRUST (recipe follows)
2/3 cup packed light brown sugar
3 tablespoons all-purpose flour
2 tablespoons cornstarch
1/2 teaspoon salt
2 1/4 cups milk
1/2 cup HERSHEY'S Syrup
3 egg yolks, well beaten
2 tablespoons butter
1 teaspoon vanilla extract
Sweetened whipped cream (optional)
Maraschino cherries (optional)
1 HERSHEY'S Milk Chocolate Bar (1.55 ounces), broken into pieces (optional)

PREPARE MACAROON-NUT CRUST.

STIR together brown sugar, flour, cornstarch and salt in medium saucepan. Gradually stir in milk, syrup and egg yolks until blended. Cook over medium heat, stirring constantly, until mixture boils; boil and stir 1 minute. Remove from heat; stir in butter and vanilla.

POUR mixture into prepared crust; place plastic wrap directly on surface. Cool on wire rack; refrigerate 6 to 8 hours. Just before serving, garnish with whipped cream, cherries and candy pieces, if desired. Cover; refrigerate leftover pie.

Makes 8 servings

MACAROON-NUT CRUST

1 1/4 cups coconut macaroon cookie crumbs (use purchased hard coconut macaroon cookies)
1/2 cup chopped walnuts
1/4 cup (1/2 stick) butter (do not use margarine), melted

HEAT oven to 350°F.

STIR together cookie crumbs, walnuts and melted butter in medium bowl. Press firmly onto bottom and up sides of 9-inch pie plate. Bake 8 to 10 minutes or until lightly browned. Cool completely.

Chocolate Syrup Mint Mousse

- 1 teaspoon unflavored gelatin
- 1 tablespoon cold water
- 2 tablespoons boiling water
- 1 cup (½ pint) cold whipping cream
- ½ cup HERSHEY'S Syrup, chilled
- 2 drops mint extract
- Whipped topping
- Sliced fresh fruit (optional)

SPRINKLE gelatin over cold water in small cup; let stand 2 minutes to soften.

ADD boiling water, stirring until gelatin is completely dissolved. Beat whipping cream in small bowl until slightly thickened; gradually add gelatin mixture, beating until stiff. Fold in syrup and mint extract.

SPOON into individual dessert dishes. Refrigerate 30 minutes or until set. Garnish with whipped topping and fruit, if desired.

Makes 4 to 6 servings

Tiramisu Temptation

- MOCHA MIXTURE (recipe follows)
- 36 (3-inch) lady fingers, split horizontally
- 3 (8-ounce) packages cream cheese or mascarpone cheese, softened
- 1 cup HERSHEY'S Syrup or HERSHEY'S SPECIAL DARK Syrup
- 1½ cups milk
- 1 package (6-serving size) vanilla instant pudding and pie mix
- 1½ cups non-dairy whipped topping
- ½ teaspoon HERSHEY'S Cocoa
- ¼ teaspoon powdered instant coffee

PREPARE MOCHA MIXTURE.

PLACE lady fingers cut side up on wax paper. Brush about ½ of MOCHA MIXTURE on surface of lady fingers. Set aside.

BEAT cream cheese and chocolate syrup until thoroughly blended in mixing bowl. Gradually blend in milk and instant pudding mix; beat 2 minutes or until slightly thickened and thoroughly blended.

GENTLY blend whipped topping into cheese mixture.

SPREAD about ¾ cup cheese mixture on bottom of 13×9×2-inch pan. Layer ⅓ of lady fingers, cut side down, over pudding. Brush lady fingers with about ⅓ of remaining MOCHA MIXTURE. Repeat layers two more times, ending with pudding layer.

STIR together cocoa and instant coffee; sprinkle over surface of dessert. Cover; refrigerate at least 8 hours.

Makes 16 to 20 servings

MOCHA MIXTURE

- ¼ cup brandy or coffee-flavored liqueur
- 3 tablespoons powdered instant coffee
- About ½ cup HERSHEY'S Syrup or HERSHEY'S SPECIAL DARK Syrup

COMBINE brandy and instant coffee in liquid measuring cup; stir until dissolved. Add syrup up to ¾ cup mark; blend.

Chocolate Syrup Swirl Dessert

CRUMB CRUST (recipe follows)
1 envelope unflavored gelatin
¼ cup cold water
1 package (8 ounces) cream cheese, softened
¼ cup sugar
1 teaspoon vanilla extract
¾ cup HERSHEY'S Syrup, chilled
¾ cup milk
VANILLA FILLING (recipe follows)
Additional HERSHEY'S Syrup (optional)

PREPARE CRUMB CRUST.

SPRINKLE gelatin over water in small saucepan; let stand 2 minutes. Cook over low heat, stirring constantly, until gelatin is dissolved.

BEAT cream cheese, sugar and vanilla in large bowl until creamy. Add syrup, gelatin mixture and milk; blend well. Refrigerate, stirring occasionally, until mixture mounds from spoon, about 20 minutes.

SPOON one-half chocolate mixture into prepared crust; top with one-half VANILLA FILLING. Repeat procedure, ending with spoonfuls of VANILLA FILLING on top. Using knife or metal spatula, gently swirl through dessert. Cover; refrigerate several hours until set. Serve with additional syrup, if desired.

Makes 10 to 12 servings

VANILLA FILLING

1 teaspoon unflavored gelatin
1 tablespoon cold water
2 tablespoons boiling water
1 cup (½ pint) cold whipping cream
2 tablespoons sugar
½ teaspoon vanilla extract

SPRINKLE gelatin over cold water in small cup; let stand 1 minute. Add boiling water; stir until gelatin is completely dissolved; cool slightly. Combine whipping cream, sugar and vanilla in medium bowl; beat until slightly thickened. Gradually add gelatin mixture; beat until stiff.

Crumb Crust: Stir together 2 cups vanilla wafer crumbs (about 60 wafers, crushed) and ⅓ cup melted butter or margarine in medium bowl. Press mixture onto bottom and 1½ inches up side of 9-inch springform pan or 10-inch pie plate. Refrigerate about 30 minutes or until firm.

Cool 'n Creamy Chocolate Pie

- 1 package (3 ounces) cream cheese, softened
- 1/4 cup sugar
- 1 teaspoon vanilla extract
- 1/2 cup HERSHEY'S Syrup
- 1 cup (1/2 pint) cold whipping cream
- 1 packaged crumb crust (6 ounces)
- Sliced fresh fruit (optional)
- Chocolate curls (optional)

BEAT cream cheese, sugar and vanilla in medium bowl until well blended. Gradually add syrup, beating until smooth. Beat whipping cream until stiff. Carefully fold into chocolate mixture. Pour into crust.

COVER; freeze until firm, about 3 hours. Just before serving, garnish with fresh fruit and chocolate curls, if desired.

Makes 6 to 8 servings

HERSHEY'S Syrup Pie

- 2 egg yolks
- 1/4 cup cornstarch
- 1/4 teaspoon salt
- 1 3/4 cups milk
- 1 cup HERSHEY'S Syrup
- 1 teaspoon vanilla extract
- 1 baked 9-inch pie crust, cooled, or packaged graham cracker crumb crust (6 ounces)
- SYRUP WHIPPED TOPPING (recipe follows)
- Fresh fruit

BEAT egg yolks in medium microwave-safe bowl. Add cornstarch, salt, milk and syrup; blend well. Microwave at MEDIUM-HIGH (70%) 6 to 8 minutes or until mixture is smooth and very thick, stirring every 2 minutes with whisk. Stir in vanilla. Pour into crust. Press plastic wrap directly onto surface.

REFRIGERATE several hours or overnight. Just before serving, garnish with SYRUP WHIPPED TOPPING and fruit. Cover; refrigerate leftover pie.

Makes 6 to 8 servings

SYRUP WHIPPED TOPPING

- 1/2 cup cold whipping cream
- 1/4 cup HERSHEY'S Syrup
- 1 tablespoon powdered sugar
- 1/4 teaspoon vanilla extract

COMBINE whipping cream, syrup, powdered sugar and vanilla in small bowl. Beat on high speed of mixer just until thickened. Use immediately.

Makes about 1 cup topping

Chocolate Mint Dessert

1 cup all-purpose flour
1 cup sugar
½ cup (1 stick) butter or margarine, softened
4 eggs
1½ cups HERSHEY'S Syrup*
MINT CREAM CENTER (recipe follows)
CHOCOLATE GLAZE (recipe follows)

One 16-ounce can HERSHEY'S Syrup contains 1½ cups syrup.

HEAT oven to 350°F. Grease 13×9×2-inch baking pan.

COMBINE flour, sugar, butter, eggs and syrup in large bowl; beat until smooth. Pour batter into prepared pan.

BAKE 25 to 30 minutes or until top springs back when touched lightly in center. Cool completely in pan on wire rack. Spread MINT CREAM CENTER on cake. Cover; refrigerate. Pour CHOCOLATE GLAZE over chilled dessert. Cover; refrigerate at least 1 hour before serving. Cover; refrigerate leftover dessert.

Makes about 12 servings

Mint Cream Center: Combine 2 cups powdered sugar, ½ cup (1 stick) softened butter or margarine and 2 tablespoons green creme de menthe (OR 1 tablespoon water plus ½ to ¾ teaspoon mint extract and 3 drops green food color may be substituted for creme de menthe) in medium bowl; beat until smooth.

Chocolate Glaze: Melt 6 tablespoons butter or margarine and 1 cup HERSHEY'S SPECIAL DARK Chocolate Chips or HERSHEY'S Semi-Sweet Chocolate Chips in small saucepan over very low heat. Remove from heat; stir until smooth. Cool slightly.

Chocolate Triangles: Cut dessert into about twelve 3-inch squares; cut each square diagonally into halves. Makes about 24 triangles.

Double Chocolate Mint Dessert: HERSHEY'S Mint Chocolate Chips may be substituted for HERSHEY'S SPECIAL DARK Chocolate Chips or HERSHEY'S Semi-Sweet Chocolate Chips in CHOCOLATE GLAZE. Omit creme de menthe in MINT CREAM CENTER.

Chocolate Peanut Butter Milkshake

- 1½ cups vanilla ice cream
- 1 cup cold milk
- ⅓ cup HERSHEY'S Syrup
- 2 tablespoons REESE'S Peanut Butter Topping or REESE'S Creamy Peanut Butter
- Whipped topping
- Maraschino cherry (optional)

PLACE ice cream, milk, syrup and topping in blender container. Cover; blend until smooth.

GARNISH with whipped topping and cherry, if desired.

Makes 2 (10-ounce) servings

Choco-Berry Cooler

- 3/4 cup cold milk
- 1/4 cup sliced fresh strawberries
- 2 tablespoons HERSHEY'S Syrup
- 2 tablespoons plus 2 small scoops vanilla ice cream, divided
- Cold ginger ale or club soda
- Fresh strawberry and mint leaves (optional)

PLACE milk, strawberries, chocolate syrup and 2 tablespoons ice cream in blender container. Cover and blend until smooth.

ALTERNATE remaining 2 scoops of ice cream and chocolate mixture in tall ice cream soda glass; fill glass with ginger ale. Garnish with a fresh strawberry and mint leaves, if desired. Serve immediately.

Variations: Before blending, substitute one of the following fruits for fresh strawberries: 3 tablespoons frozen strawberries with syrup, thawed; 1/2 peeled fresh peach or 1/3 cup canned peach slices; 2 slices canned pineapple or 1/4 cup canned crushed pineapple; 1/4 cup sweetened fresh raspberries or 3 tablespoons frozen raspberries with syrup, thawed.

Makes 1 (14-ounce) servings

Chocolate Cherry Milkshake

- 4 scoops (about 2 cups) vanilla ice cream or frozen yogurt
- ¾ cup cold milk
- ¼ cup HERSHEY'S Syrup
- 8 maraschino cherries, stems removed
- Whipped topping and additional cherry (optional)

PLACE ice cream, milk, syrup and cherries in blender container. Cover; blend until smooth.

GARNISH with whipped topping and cherry, if desired.

Makes 2 (10-ounce) servings

Peachy Chocolate Yogurt Shake

- 2/3 cup peeled fresh peach slices or 1 package (10 ounces) frozen peach slices, thawed and drained
- 1/4 teaspoon almond extract
- 2 cups (1 pint) vanilla nonfat frozen yogurt
- 1/4 cup HERSHEY'S Syrup
- 1/4 cup nonfat milk

PLACE peaches and almond extract in blender container. Cover; blend until smooth.

ADD frozen yogurt, syrup and milk. Cover; blend until smooth. Serve immediately.

Makes 4 servings

Strawberry Pink Lemonade

- 1 can (6 ounces) frozen lemonade concentrate, partially thawed
- 2⅔ cups cold water
- ⅓ cup HERSHEY'S Strawberry Syrup

STIR together lemonade concentrate, water and syrup in pitcher. Serve in tall glasses over crushed ice.

Makes about 4 servings or 1 quart lemonade

Strawberry Pink Lemonade Ice Pops: Stir together lemonade concentrate, water and syrup as directed above. Divide mixture among 8 paper cold drink cups (5 ounces each). Freeze about 1 hour; insert wooden popsicle sticks into strawberry mixture. Cover; freeze until firm. Peel off cups to serve. **Makes 8 pops.**

Single Serving: Place about 1½ tablespoons strawberry syrup in bottom of tall glass. Fill with ice. Pour lemonade over ice. Stir to blend or serve with long spoon for blending.

Iced Cappuccino

- $^2/_3$ cup HERSHEY'S Syrup, chilled
- 2 cups cold coffee
- 2 cups vanilla ice cream
- Ice cubes or crushed ice
- Whipped topping (optional)
- Ground cinnamon (optional)

PLACE syrup and coffee in blender container; cover and blend on high speed. Add ice cream; cover and blend until smooth.

SERVE immediately over ice; top with whipped topping and ground cinnamon, if desired.

Makes 6 (6-ounce) servings

Lower Fat Iced Cappuccino: Follow above directions using reduced-fat vanilla ice cream and fat-free whipped topping.

Cappuccino Cooler

- 1½ cups cold coffee
- 1½ cups chocolate ice cream
- ¼ cup HERSHEY'S Syrup
- Crushed ice
- Whipped cream
- Ground cinnamon (optional)

COMBINE coffee, ice cream and syrup in blender container. Cover; blend until smooth. Serve immediately over crushed ice. Garnish with whipped cream and cinnamon, if desired.

Makes about 4 servings

Variation: Substitute vanilla ice cream for chocolate; increase syrup to ⅓ cup.